A QUESTRON® ELECTRONIC WORKBOOK

PRESCHOOL SKILLS

PRICE/STERN/SLOAN
Publishers, Inc., Los Angeles

DISTRIBUTED BY
RANDOM HOUSE, INC.
New York

THE QUESTRON® SYSTEM
COMBINING FUN WITH LEARNING

This book is part of **THE QUESTRON SYSTEM**, which offers children a unique aid to learning and endless hours of challenging entertainment.

The QUESTRON electronic "wand" uses a microchip to sense correct and incorrect answers with "right" or "wrong" sounds and lights. Victory sounds and lights reward the user when particular sets of questions or games are completed. Powered by a nine-volt alkaline battery, which is activated only when the wand is pressed on a page, QUESTRON should have an exceptionally long life. The QUESTRON ELECTRONIC WAND can be used with any book in the QUESTRON series.

A note to parents...

With QUESTRON, right or wrong answers are indicated instantly and can be tried over and over to reinforce learning and improve skills. Children need not be restricted to the books designated for their age group, as interests and rates of development vary widely. Also, within many of the books, certain pages are designed for the older end of the age group and will provide a stimulating challenge to younger children.

Many activities are designed at different levels. For example, the child can select an answer by recognizing a letter or by reading an entire word. The activities for pre-readers and early readers are intended to be used with parental assistance. Interaction with parents or older children will stimulate the learning experience.

QUESTRON Project Director: Roger Burrows
Educational Consultants: Verna Burnett, Beverley Dietz
Writers: Susan Parker Lewis, Rozanne Lanczak Williams
Illustrators: Klaus Björkman, Michael Bonner
Graphic Designers: Judy Walker, Lee A. Scott

Copyright ©1985 by Price/Stern/Sloan Publishers, Inc. All rights reserved under International and Pan-American Copyright Conventions. No part of this publication may be reproduced, stored in a retrieval system, or transmitted in any form or by any means, electronic, mechanical, photocopying, recording or otherwise, without the prior written permission of the publisher. Published by Price/Stern/Sloan Publishers, Inc., 410 North La Cienega Boulevard, Los Angeles, California 90048. Distributed by Random House, Inc., 201 East 50th Street, New York, New York 10022.   ISBN: 0-394-87702-0
3 4 5 6 7 8 9 0

QUESTRON® is a trademark of Price/Stern/Sloan Publishers, Inc. U.S.A.
U.S. Patent 4,604,065; U.S. Patent 4,627,819; U.S. Patent Pending.
Canada Patented/Brevete 1984. International Patents Pending.
Printed in the United States of America.

HOW TO START QUESTRON

Hold **QUESTRON** at this angle and press the activator button firmly on the page.

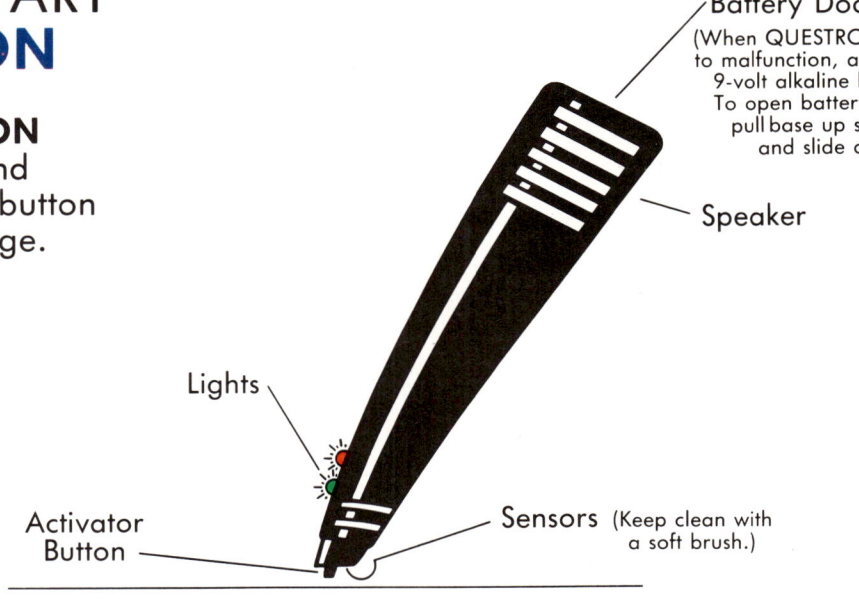

Battery Door (When QUESTRON begins to malfunction, add a new 9-volt alkaline battery. To open battery door, pull base up slightly and slide out.)

Speaker

Lights

Activator Button

Sensors (Keep clean with a soft brush.)

HOW TO USE QUESTRON

PRESS
Press **QUESTRON** firmly on the shape below, then lift it off.

TRACK
Press **QUESTRON** down on "Start" and keep it pressed down as you move to "Finish."

RIGHT & WRONG WITH QUESTRON

Press **QUESTRON** on the square.

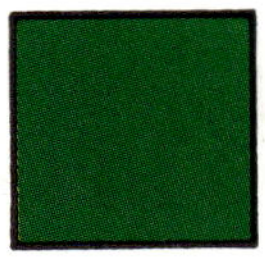

See the green light and hear the sound. This green light and sound say "You are correct."

Press **QUESTRON** on the triangle.

The red light and sound say "Try again." Lift **QUESTRON** off the page and wait for the sound to stop.

Press **QUESTRON** on the circle.

Hear the victory sound. Don't be dazzled by the flashing lights. You deserve them.

Monster Search

There are **10** monsters at the carnival. Press **Questron** on each monster.

Skill: Visual perception

Monster Maze

Help the monster find a friend. Press **Questron** on the footprints that belong to the missing monster.

Skill: Visual discrimination and motor coordination

Flower Power

Help the two friends find the castle. Track **Questron** on the path with the flowers that are the same as the one the monster is holding. Start on the ★.

Skill: Visual discrimination and motor coordination

Me and My Shadow

Look at the shadow in the first box in each row. Press **Questron** on the monster or monsters in that row that match the shadow.

Skill: Visual discrimination / similarities

My Shadow and Me

Look at the shadow in the first box in each row. Press **Questron** on the monster or monsters in that row that do not match the shadow.

Skill: Visual discrimination / differences

Monster Match

Track **Questron** on the path that shows groups of monsters that are the **same** as each other. Start on the ★.

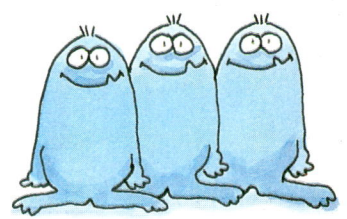

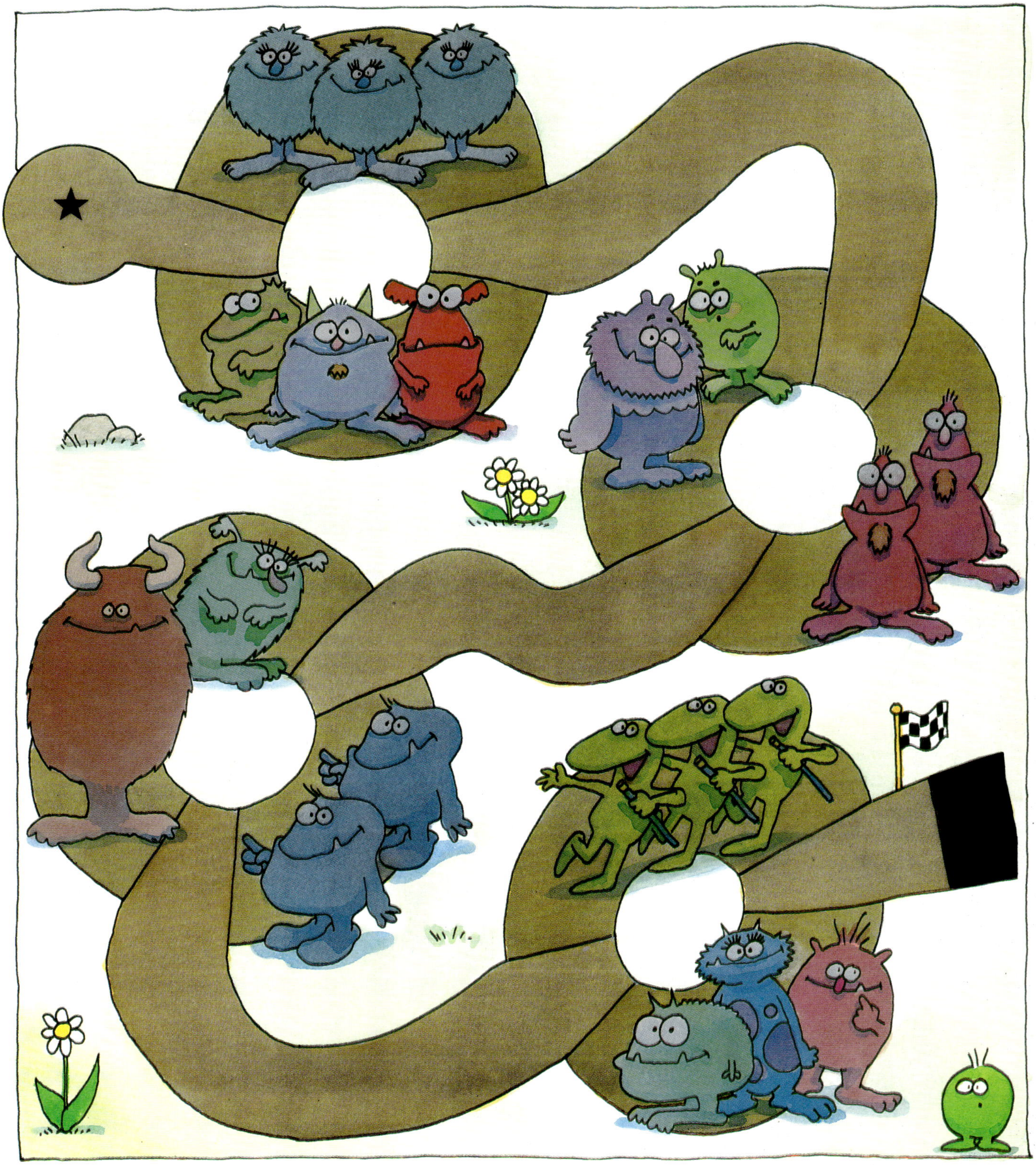

Skill: Visual discrimination / similarities

What's Missing?

There is something missing from each picture. Track **Questron** to what is missing. Start on the ★.

Skill: Visual perception

What can you **taste**?

What can you **touch**?

Good Foods

Press **Questron** on the square inside each picture that shows **food** that is good for you.

Skill: Life skills / recognizing healthy foods

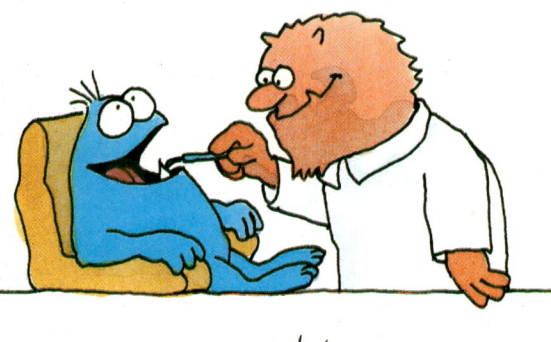

Good Habits

Press **Questron** on the square inside each picture that shows a **habit** that is good for you.

Skill: Life skills / recognizing good health practices

Safety First

Look at the pictures in each row.
Press **Questron** on the square inside
each picture that shows a **safe** activity.

Skill: Life skills / recognizing safe activities

Monsters at Work

What does each monster use at work?
Track **Questron** to the correct answer. Start on the ★.

Skill: Identifying tools and occupations

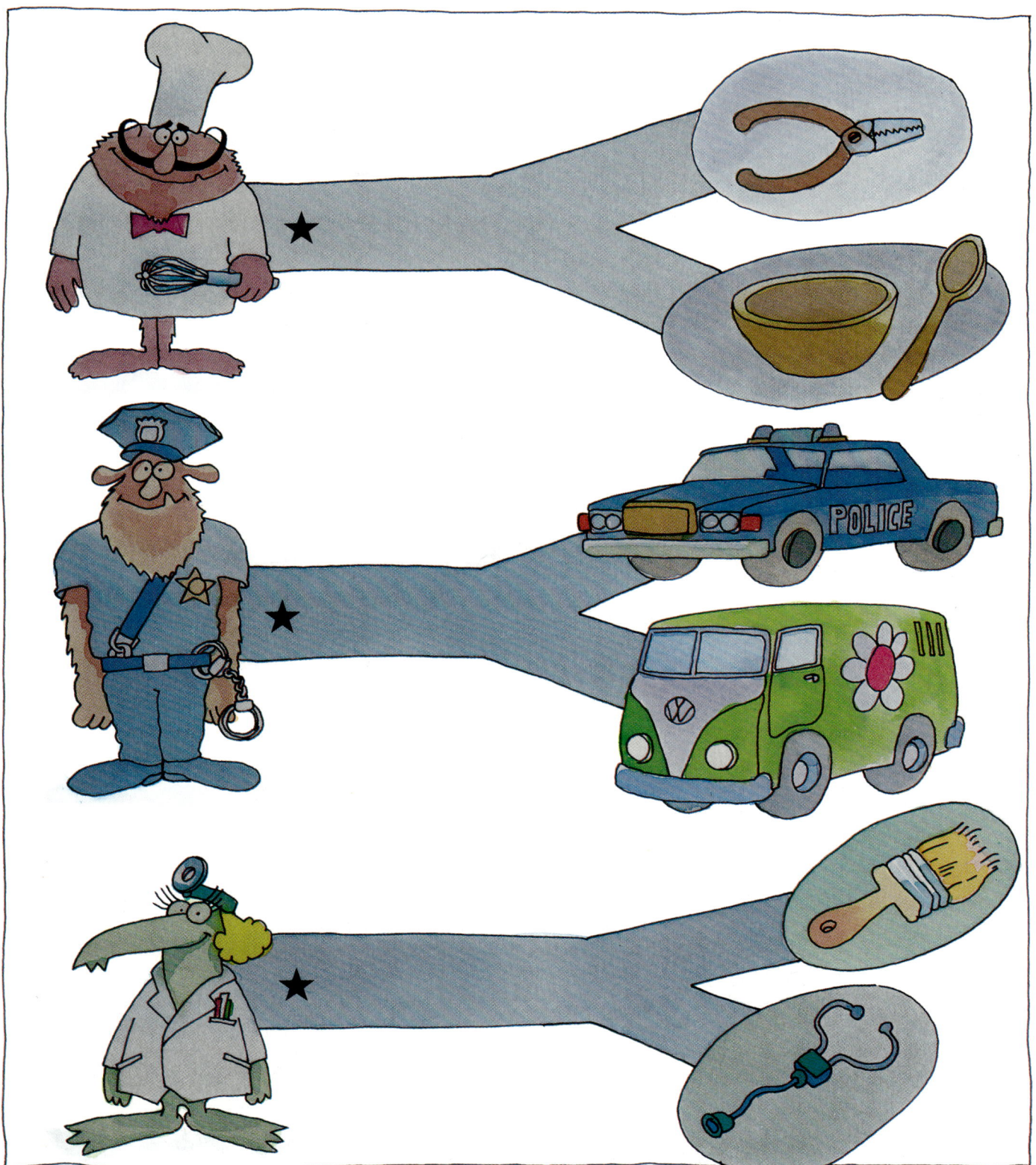

Dressing Up

Track **Questron** on the path that shows the things you can **wear**. Start on the ★.

Skill: Classification / clothing

Chowing Down

Track **Questron** on the path that shows the things you can **eat**. Start on the ★.

Skill: Classification / foods

Monsters at School

Look at the top picture. Press **Questron** on the things in the bottom picture that belong in the classroom.

Skill: Classification / things that belong

Monsters at Play

Look at the top picture. Press **Questron** on the things in the bottom picture that belong on the playground.

Skill: Classification / things that belong

31

THE QUESTRON LIBRARY OF ELECTRONIC BOOKS

A series of books specially designed to reach—and teach—and entertain children of all ages

QUESTRON ELECTRONIC WORKBOOKS

Early Childhood

My First Counting Book
My First ABC Book
My First Book of Animals
Shapes and Sizes
Preschool Skills
My First Vocabulary
My First Nursery Rhymes
Reading Readiness
My First Words
My First Numbers
Going Places
Kindergarten Skills
Sesame Street® 1 to 10
Sesame Street® A to Z
Autos, Ships, Trains and Planes

Grades K–5

My First Reading Book (K–1)
Little Miss™ — First School Days (K–2)
Mr. Men™ — A First Reading Adventure (K–2)
Word Games (K–2)
My First Book of Telling Time (K–2)
Day of the Dinosaur (K–3)
First Grade Skills (1)
My First Book of Addition (1–2)
Bigger, Smaller, Shorter, Taller… (1–3)
The Storytime Activity Book (1–3)
My Robot Book (1–3)
My First Book of Spelling (1–3)
My First Book of Subtraction (1–3)
My First Book of Multiplication (2–3)
I Want to Be… (2–5)
Number Fun (2–5)
Word Fun (2–5)

Electronic Quizbooks for the Whole Family

Trivia Fun and Games
How, Why, Where and When
More How, Why, Where and When
World Records and Amazing Facts

The Princeton Review S.A.T.® Program

The Princeton Review: S.A.T.® Math
The Princeton Review: S.A.T.® Verbal

PRICE/STERN/SLOAN — **RANDOM HOUSE, INC.**
Publishers, Inc., Los Angeles   New York

CW 1/87